# Plunder Darkness
An Experiential Journey

# Advance Praise For Plunder Darkness
## An Experiential Journey

"When I first met Craig Muster, I immediately recognized his pursuit of the uncommon. As I partnered with him I saw his drive to destroy the works of the devil and to plunder darkness. Now, we have his secrets of gaining and maintaining daily victory at our fingertips. Craig has taken ancient technologies and given them to us in a pragmatic daily victory process. If you desire to plunder fear, awkwardness, and doubt and reap the rewards of hope, joy, love, and prosperity, this daily action plan is going to change your life. Thank you Craig for sharing victory secrets in "Plunder Darkness."

**Sincerely yours,**
**Tracey Armstrong**
*Founder, Citadel Churches*
*Best selling author of "Followership" and "The Experimentalist"*
*www.traceyarmstrong.com*
*www.citadelchurch.com*

"The journey God has called each one of us to is never accomplished on our own but requires the strength and help of others. I'm grateful for the men and women that have come alongside me in my journey and have helped me mine the gold in my life. Craig Muster has been that person for so many people who have longed to achieve the things on their heart. Plunder Darkness is Craig doing what he does best, helping people discover the greatness God has placed inside of them. In a practical and yet powerful format, this 21-day journey will strengthen and equip you for all God has called you to."

**Banning Leibscher**
*Founding Pastor of Jesus Culture*
*Author of The Three-Mile Walk*

"The extraordinary combination of being a seasoned minister, a passionate worship leader, and experienced life-coach makes Craig one of the most dynamic teacher's I've had the privilege of knowing. He is gifted at drawing the gold out of everyone he encounters & equipping them with tools for a life of courageous boldness. Craig also has a unique ability to enliven the context of scripture against the backdrop of our modern day to day life. As a true friend of Jesus, he provokes his audience to delve further into the meaning of already profound biblical stories which unlocks fresh understanding of spiritual truths. With Craig as your guide, this 21 day experience will be rich with discovery and exploration of the spacious places and victories that God has designed for you!"

**Tiffany Buhler**
*Managing Director*
*David's Tent*
*www.davidstent.net*

"Craig Muster has developed a book that is inspirational and practical. It is organized in such a way that you feel drawn into your own story as you find yourself in conversations with God. Plunder Darkness also contains nuggets of wisdom that function as mirrors into the depths of the soul: we can see ourselves clearly, and with that clarity comes real hunger, deeper trust and a more meaningful life. His ability to put wise concepts into understandable language is a testimony to his communication skills. "Plunder Darkness" is well worth the read.

**Scott Smith**
*Church Planter*
*Missionary To Spain*
*www.scottmarisa.com*

"Plunder Darkness empowers you to suspend your fear of the dark. Craig Muster's insights equip you to embrace your moments of darkness and turn them into hope, sparking a fire back in your soul that'll light up the darkest of caves. A breakthrough paradigm awaits as you partner with the Holy Spirit to face the fears and shame that have kept you imprisoned in your deepest darkness."

Steve Chua
*Executive Life Coach*
*www.stevechuaintl.com*

"I'm convinced that Craig Muster must have been writing his new *Plunder Darkness: An Experiential Journey* just for me. Each chapter compels you to consider a way of looking at life through the lens of authenticity that reflects hopeful change. If applied, this journal will help to reconcile areas of your life's journey that have at times hijacked your peace and passion for Jesus and His Kingdom. Give Jesus permission to plunder every area of your life that has held you back from experiencing all the benefits of identifying as a son or daughter of the Most High. Happy plundering!"

Barry Sappington-
*Lead Pastor- Crosspointe Life Church*
*Executive Life Coach @ Sappington Coaching*
*www.sappingtoncoaching.org*

"As a leader I have found that I need to be sharpened and encouraged by leaders, ministers, and authors who have truly walked the walk. Craig Muster has written an incredible book that forced me to confront areas in my own spiritual life as well as my vision and capacity for leadership. Have you ever wondered why you have not been able to see breakthrough or advancement in your life? Plunder Darkness will take you on a journey with the Holy Spirit that will require you to question presuppositions, hindrances, and obstacles to seeing you live and thrive as the Lord has destined you."

Rev. Jason Holland
*President - Joshua Nations*
*www.joshuanations.org*

"In Plunder Darkness Craig takes you into the role of a miner looking for gold where no one else suspects it to be found!

Craig has the ability not only as a Coach but as an author to go deep down the mine shaft to help us pull out "every ounce of treasure shrouded by the natural eye"! As a good friend, Craig helps me Plunder Darkness every time I am with him!"

Prepare yourselves to descend into the mine shaft and "PLUNDER DARKNESS"

**Rick Sainz**
*Senior Leader- Red Seal Ministries*
*www.redsealministries.com*

"I was there when Craig Muster first spoke on Plunder Darkness. It was life-changing. It has stayed with me for years and I now use it to help others to this very day. It will stay with you as well. There are moments in life where we encounter God and it changes us forever. This isn't a normal book---it is supernatural. You will receive a God "moment" in your life that will change you as you go through this book. Prepare your heart to receive and be willing to Plunder the Darkness with God."

**Brae Wyckoff**
*President of Kingdom Creativity International,*
*Director of Kingdom Writers Association,*
*Award-winning Amazon bestselling author*
*www.kingdomwritersassociation.com*

# Plunder Darkness
## An Experiential Journey

Plunder Darkness

**An Experiential Journey**

Copyright © 2021 by Craig D Muster

All rights reserved. No part of this book may be reproduced or used in any manner without written permission of the copyright owner except for the use of quotations in a book review. For more information, address: craig@craigmuster.com

FIRST EDITION

ISBN: 9798707207204

www.craigmuster.com

Scripture quotations taken from the Amplified® Bible (AMPC),

Copyright © 1954, 1958, 1962, 1964, 1965, 1987 by The Lockman Foundation

Used by permission.

Scripture taken from the New King James Version®. Copyright © 1982 by Thomas Nelson, Inc. Used by permission. All rights reserved.

THE HOLY BIBLE, NEW INTERNATIONAL VERSION®, NIV® Copyright © 1973, 1978, 1984, 2011 by Biblica, Inc.™ Used by permission. All rights reserved worldwide.

Scripture quotations marked TPT are from The Passion Translation®. Copyright © 2017, 2018 by Passion & Fire Ministries, Inc. Used by permission. All rights reserved. ThePassionTranslation.com.

# Dedication

I dedicate this book to my wife and best friend Karlet Muster, who has walked this journey with me for almost 20 years now. Your love for God and lifestyle of complete surrender still astounds me. I am even more in love with you today than the day you said, "I do"! The adventure has just begun.

I also dedicate this book to my three children. Know this, you are the reason I fight to live from my heart, to fully engage with love and to live this life to the fullest! I love you so much!

# Contents

The Journey Begins: 21 Days to Plunder Darkness .................. 1
Day 1: Plunder Your Moment with Jesus ................. 5
Day 2: Plunder Awkwardness .................. 9
Day 3: Plunder Vulnerability .................. 13
Day 4: Plunder Hopelessness .................. 17
Day 5: Plunder Possibility .................. 21
Day 6: Plunder Your Thirst .................. 25
Day 7: Plunder the Fear of Being Known .................. 29
Day 8: Plunder Hope Fulfilled .................. 33
Day 9: Plunder Unconditional Love .................. 37
Day 10: Plunder Jealousy .................. 41
Day 11: Plunder Rejection .................. 45
Day 12: Plunder Meaninglessness .................. 49
Day 13: Plunder Potential Bitterness .................. 53
Day 14: Plunder Turmoil .................. 57
Day 15: Plunder Tension .................. 61
Day 16: Plunder the Mundane .................. 65
Day 17: Plunder Delay .................. 69
Day 18: Plunder Brokenness .................. 73
Day 19: Plunder Pressure .................. 77
Day 20: Plunder Disappointment In Dreams .................. 81
Day 21: Plunder Pain .................. 85
The Journey Continues .................. 89
About the Author .................. 93

# The Journey Begins
# 21 Days to Plunder Darkness

---

I ONCE HEARD A story of a gold mine in Nevada that yielded a substantial amount of gold for decades, then dwindled to next to nothing. The price to continue digging became greater than the potential to find more gold, so the mine was shut down, leaving large mountains of useless dirt and many empty mine shafts that had run their course.

Then someone discovered that cyanide could extract micro particles of gold out of dirt. This changed everything! Now miners had the capacity to take large amounts of seemingly useless dirt and filter it through a solution made of cyanide. The result was stunning. The smallest particles of gold were now valuable enough to mine.

A poison—cyanide—best known for its ability to kill was now the tool used to mine for gold. And piles of meaningless dirt became mountains of potential riches!

What happened with this gold mine is the perfect metaphor for what God wants to do with you over the next twenty-one days. In short, He wants to show you how the "poison" that has sought to derail your *fullest life* can become the greatest tool in discovering the riches your heart has been longing for!

## Plunder Darkness: An Experiential Journey

*Plunder Darkness* is an Experiential Journey that invites you to venture into the deepest places of seeming "darkness" in your life and pull out every ounce of treasure shrouded from the natural eye. It's time to mine those dirt piles once more. It's time to *plunder darkness!*

You were born to live a supernatural life. You were born to see what others can't see, to go places others avoid, and to do feats that just yesterday even you thought impossible! Darkness would love to define your possibilities in life. It would like to tell you where you can and can't go and what you can and can't do. It wants to shade your past, future, and present with hopelessness, apathy, and sorrow. But God has something else to say about the issue. The book of Psalms describes God in great depth as being superior to any darkness:

> Even the darkness will not be dark to You; the night will shine like the day, for darkness is as light to You. (Psalm 139:12 NIV)

God flips the script on the ultimate purpose of darkness. He takes that which we've been running from, stands it in front of us, and invites us to mine it for our deepest treasures. That is the power of redemption—our weakness in His strength, our sorrow in His comfort, our pain in His care, and our fear in the hands of His faith.

Buckle up and do what you were made to do—explore the unknown, venture beyond your comfort zone, dig deep into the recesses of your soul, become the best version of yourself ... and *plunder darkness*!

Over the next twenty-one days, we will be unpacking wisdom and tools from the following texts of Scripture:

## The Journey Begins: 21 Days to Plunder Darkness

Days 1-9: *John 4:1-42*
Days 10-21: *Genesis 37, 39-45*

I encourage you to read the entire text of Scripture related to each section of the Experiential Journal before you start. This will enable you to see hidden treasure that might not even be covered in the book.

Remember, this is intended to be a conversation between you and God. He loves sharing personal insights of your story through His eyes. After all, His version of your story is the ultimate truth of who you are. Every other version is a cheap copy. He is the Restorer, and His greatest work is crafted in those who've lost hope but still surrender, who've lost innocence but still receive mercy, who've lost purpose but still respond to His voice speaking their name once more. So, if you find yourself getting distracted and drawn into a conversation with the Father, Jesus, and the Holy Spirit while you're reading, go with it. That's the point. By all means, *go with it*!

But whatever you do, make sure you journal something every day. Oftentimes what you might think of as *insignificant* becomes the *deepest thread of truth* once you see the whole story.

The time has come to start your pilgrimage. It's time to *plunder darkness*!

# Journal

# DAY 1
## Plunder Your Moment with Jesus

---

A woman of Samaria came to draw water. Jesus said to her, "Give Me a drink." (John 4:7 NKJV)

*Maridhia is a Swahili name meaning "satisfied."*
*I have chosen to use this name for the woman at the well.*

"GIVE ME A drink." Why is Jesus asking Maridhia for anything? Jesus is fully God and fully human. As a human, He had real "felt," everyday needs, like you and I do. But He could have gone with His disciples to town and gotten a drink Himself. Instead, He chooses to stay at a well where He is at the mercy of a Samaritan woman's generosity.

In general, most of us try to position ourselves where we don't need anyone else's help. Yet Jesus opens the whole encounter with this request, a need. It seems counterintuitive. We know the Messiah came to save the lost and bring the kingdom in all its glory. Why start the conversation with a request? Why not perform a miracle right off the bat? Display His power and authority? There has to be something here we're not seeing.

Jesus knows exactly what He's doing. Even today, God still

positions us to *matter* to Him. Our actions, our desires, and our decisions all play an incredible part in His plan. One would think that if God wanted to be certain everything turned out according to His plan, then He would simply control us and leave no room for our error. Instead, He's made room for our mistakes, which means there is also room for our victories to matter as well! But victories don't come without surrender. And Jesus loves to draw us out of hiding and into surrender by making simple requests.

Simple requests of Jesus can alter your course indefinitely. Vulnerability begins to shatter the jaded areas of your soul as the King of Kings asks *you* for something. You? Yep. He is the King of Kings. The Alpha and Omega. The Prince of Peace. His Name is above all names. Yet, sometimes it's not what He speaks to you that begins the shift. Sometimes the change starts in what He wants from you, something you can give Him right now.

I dare ask—do you have something He wants? Is He taking the time to hang out with you right now? Is He starting the conversation with, "Give me *that*"? See, you might not have much, but He still would like to have it—not to deprive you of it, but to make room for what you bring. What you give to Him makes a difference. He's not patronizing you when He asks for your help. He's inviting you into a friendship where you give and receive.

Will you say yes? No matter how insignificant or significant His request, will you say yes? If so, take some time to contemplate. Imagine Him coming to you and asking you for what He wants. Imagine yourself holding it out and giving it to Him. Then let Him take you somewhere you've never gone.

**Plunder Your Moment with Jesus.**

# Journal

# DAY 2
# Plunder Awkwardness

---

> Then the woman of Samaria said to Him, "How is it that You, being a Jew, ask a drink from me, a Samaritan woman?" For Jews have no dealings with Samaritans. (John 4:9 NKJV)

AWKWARD CONVERSATIONS SHOULD be avoided at all costs—right? I mean, I personally hate it when I feel trapped in an awkward conversation. Some people thrive on that kind of stuff, but not me. I'd rather spend my time with people who are certain to enjoy my company. Hanging out with someone who more than likely is disgusted with me is not my idea of a good afternoon. And going through all the *have to's* of politeness feels like a waste of time. Yet, Jesus goes out of His way to have a conversation with someone who in all likelihood will be hostile, or at best, indifferent. The Samaritans had been kicked around by the Jews for so long that deep contempt flowed both ways. Jesus cuts right through it. He's not afraid of rejection. His peace must have been deafening to Maridhia.

Why does God love to offend our comfort zones? Shocking our "normals" is part of His "normal." Throwing cold water in the face of our comfort—that's what it takes sometimes to wake us up to the reality that He wants to have a conversation with us. Not with our façade, but with *us*! Jesus' truth cuts through all the tension built up through years of fear and self-preservation. Before we have a chance to put on the face we know is "acceptable" to Him, He shows up. Before we change our clothes to look like Him, He shows up. Before we have time to rehearse what we'll say, He shows up. Or even if we did rehearse, some of us stink at playing the role, and out of our mouth comes exactly how we're actually doing. And you know what? He shows up!

God loves to be with us. He loves to be with *you*! I mean, He died to be with you. Don't let the cultural barriers get in the way. Don't let your sin get in the way. Don't let your past get in the way. Don't let your perceived future get in the way. When He speaks, don't let the awkwardness of your dysfunction keep you from having a chat. Just try talking to Him and see where it leads. You might find yourself enjoying this awkward conversation more than any other conversation you've had in the past.

**Plunder Awkwardness.**

# Journal

# DAY 3
## Plunder Vulnerability

---

Jesus answered and said to her, "If you knew the gift of God, and who it is who says to you, 'Give Me a drink,' you would have asked Him, and He would have given you living water." (John 4:10 NKJV)

Have you ever found yourself talking to God without really knowing who He was? Startling, I know—but common. In fact, for the rest of our lives we'll be talking to a God we are intimately close to yet barely know. No matter how near we draw to God or how much time we spend with Him, He is so much more than our imaginations can grasp. It's what makes this relationship with Him so amazing and terrifying at the same time.

We are so far from being able to control God. Since our imagination likes to promise security in things we believe we can control, our inability to control God can be quite disconcerting. But that's also where the wonder sneaks in. There is no wonder in something we've figured out. But it will take eternity to discover the surface of God's complexity—that demands wonder!

What's more mind-blowing is that this eternally complex God

invites us to get to know Him one day at a time. "If you knew who it is … you would ask." The implication is, "Come get to know Me. In getting to know Me you'll know Who I am for you and what you can expect to receive from Me."

How freeing it is to be in a relationship with a God we cannot manipulate but can come close to. His sheer strength is ultimately felt in our deepest psyche when we come to grips with the nature of this uncontrollable God. He is for us, not against us. He is a good God. That's the reality that soothes our hearts and enables us to sneak in so close to Him we can hear His heartbeat.

Being introduced to His wonder changes us. Staying rooted in wonder transforms us. No matter how much we know about Him there is still so much more to see, feel, hear, and taste. Who is He really? Take another look. He'll show you something you've never seen before.

Crazy invitation. Crazier promise! He not only invites us to know Him, He invites us to ask Him for that for which we thirst, then He promises to give it to us! As we initially draw near to God our thirst doesn't leave—it gets clarified. The closer we are to Him, the more we know what we really need. It's at that moment we can find the courage to ask for it.

**Plunder Vulnerability.**

# Journal

# DAY 4
## Plunder Hopelessness

---

> The woman replied, "But sir, you don't even have a bucket and this well is very deep. So where do you find this 'living water'? Do you really think that you are greater than our ancestor Jacob who dug this well and drank from it himself, along with his children and livestock?" (John 4:11-12 11 TPT)

FROM MARIDHIA'S PERSPECTIVE, there wasn't any reasonable or foreseeable way of Jesus making good on His promise. And she lets Him know how absurd His promise sounds. Maridhia knew who Jacob was. She revered Jacob and his faith. Jacob was a hero to this woman. But Jacob had his own limitations, and Jacob's well couldn't fulfill what Jesus had promised. This water did not seem to be "living." No matter how many times she drank from this well she still felt dry, hopeless, and dead inside. So how could Jesus promise to give her something Jacob could not? Her reasoning appears to provoke her to "push" back against Jesus' promise.

God's promises have a tendency to offend us anywhere we've given up hope. We try and find something that will bring the dead inside of us back to life, only to realize there isn't a permanent solution. So we try to do our best and put one foot in front of the other. Then Jesus shows up and disrupts our routine with a promise, and instead of bringing comfort, it seems to first disrupt our "peace." Why? Because we've finally found a little peace in letting go of the hope that anything will ever change. So when He says, "Hey, that thing you need—I have it," our first response can be, "Seriously? Don't promise something You can't back up. False hope is worse than no hope."

Jesus doesn't mind the questions of the heart. They don't keep Him from butting into our business and using "hope" to disrupt our normal. He does it anyways and doesn't even feel bad about it. Our initial challenge to His promise doesn't disqualify us from a conversation with Him.

So, do you have somewhere in your life that God is attempting to bring hope back to? Maybe somewhere you'd just as soon leave in the grave? Maybe He's already whispered a promise you're pretending you didn't hear. It might just be too painful to think much about. But why not take a moment to continue the conversation, even if you find yourself pushing back? "God, how do You think You can do this? My whole past shouts that it is impossible, even for You?" He won't be offended. But He might have His own perspective on the subject.

**Plunder Hopelessness.**

# Journal

# DAY 5
# Plunder Possibility

---

Jesus answered, "If you drink from Jacob's well you'll be thirsty again and again, but if anyone drinks the living water I give them, they will never thirst again and will be forever satisfied! For when you drink the water I give you it becomes a gushing fountain *of the Holy Spirit*, springing up and flooding you with endless life!" (John 4:13-14 TPT)

"IF" IS A word that denotes options. "If you drink the same water you've been drinking then nothing will change. If you drink the water I have for you then everything will change." Jesus possesses exactly what Maridhia wants the most. But there is still an "if" involved.

Have you noticed that God never forces someone to receive what He has for them? He has such a tremendous respect for our ability to make our own decisions. He cheers us on. He invites us in. Never forces Himself on us. But He does whet our appetite for what He has in mind for us. God is brilliant at that. His methods are as unique to the person He's talking to as to the situation they might find themselves in. But make no mistake—Jesus is a genius! So while He won't make the decision for her, He will definitely massage her appetite for what He promises.

But how could this be true? She had drunk from Jacob's well many times before, only to find her thirst return rather quickly. And now Jesus is claiming that what He has to offer will so satisfy her that she won't have to return? Not ending there, He promises the absurd. Not only will she not have to keep trying to fill her own void with pathetic imitations of love, but something will begin to bubble out of her transforming the community around her.

When I first come to God with a need or a request, nine out of ten times it is for something less than what He really has for me. But at least it's a starting point. He loves to hear what's on my mind—and what's on your mind. If I try to get it perfect before I say anything to Him, then I probably won't say anything. But listening to Him, taking the time to really listen even as He's taken the time to listen to me, that's when I hear the audacious promises He's stored up for me. Only then am I profoundly overwhelmed by Him. It's the overwhelming that transforms me.

With Maridhia, Jesus is promising something so outlandish that she will have no choice but to either completely jump in or completely jump back. What is God currently promising you that has an "if" attached to it? I know it can be scary to think about. But the price of not entertaining His thoughts might be too high to bear.

**Plunder Possibility.**

# Journal

# DAY 6
# Plunder Your Thirst

---

The woman replied, "Let me drink that water so I'll never be thirsty again and won't have to come back here to draw water." (John 4:15 TPT)

CERTAINTY. WE ALL want it. Sometimes we're willing to pay any price to have certainty. In stark contrast, Maridhia reached out past her innate need for it.

Imagine yourself in her sandals. She meets this Man for the first time. He's a Jew. He starts up a confusing conversation with her, but something in her heart stays engaged. Jesus then makes a crazy claim—He has water that will exponentially satisfy her thirst!

What would you do if you were in her story? Ask for proof? Check Jesus' credentials? Maybe wait a couple minutes to see if this all made sense? I don't know. But I might've gotten as far away from Jesus as possible at that point. Strange people make strange promises.

I'm so glad Maridhia didn't follow my route. Instead, she went headlong into asking Jesus for what He said He could give her! I love that. She didn't yet have understanding, but she was thirsty.

Her thirst won out before her doubts took over, and so she found herself standing before Jesus asking Him for exactly what He promised.

What has God promised you that you still don't fully understand? Are you waiting for understanding before you say "yes"? You might be waiting a long time. Some understanding doesn't come until *after* we say yes.

I encourage you right now to take a moment to revisit God's "out of your world" promises—the ones that your brain still hiccups over. What if He were standing in front of you now, promising once again to give you exactly what you need? Do you dare say, "Yes! Give me some of that! I might not understand it, but I know I want it."

Thirst always points to something. So when your thirst is driving you into God, it's time to yield to it. Turn your affections toward Him right now and remind yourself of your thirst that only He can quench.

**Plunder Your Thirst.**

# Journal

# DAY 7
# Plunder the Fear of Being Known

---

Jesus said, "Go get your husband and bring him back here."

"But I'm not married," the woman answered.

"That's true," Jesus said, "for you've been married five times and now you're living with a man who is not your husband. You have told the truth."

The woman said, "You must be a prophet! So tell me this: Why do our fathers worship God here on this nearby mountain, but your people teach that Jerusalem is the place where we must worship. Which is right?" (John 4:16-18 TPT)

O*UCH. T*HAT'S WHAT went through my head when I read this verse. "Get your husband and bring him back here"? *That's the response, Jesus? Maridhia asks for what You promised. Why play games? You said You'd give her water. She said, "Okay, give me some." But instead of giving it to her, You ask her to do something that is impossible for her to do?*

I wonder what thoughts raced through her head as she

considered how to respond to Jesus' prerequisite to Him quenching her thirst. She decides on giving Him the factual truth without giving away her whole story: "But I'm not married."

Will Jesus look the other way, or will He go deeper? He'll go deeper of course! "You've been married five times and the man you're living with isn't even your husband."

The profoundness of this exchange isn't that Jesus reveals He knows her past, but that she doesn't run away in shame when He does! There must have been something in His eyes that said His compassion was stronger than her failures. So, instead of running she actually draws even closer to Him and eases into an even deeper conversation. She responds, "You must be a prophet," then asks Him to clarify something very close to her heart concerning worship. This isn't a woman trying to close herself off to Jesus. Maridhia is looking for an excuse to go "all in" in getting closer to Him. Love is that powerful. Somewhere in this exchange, Maridhia is experiencing love. But it's not coming in the way we would imagine.

Jesus is a master at peeling back the layers of self-preservation in which we've wrapped ourselves. He'll ask us questions—not so that He can finally know the truth about us, but so that we can finally know the truth about ourselves, and more importantly, the truth about Him.

There is a line to an old song ringing in my head as I write this: "The One who knows you best loves you most." We tend to believe it is, "The one who knows the good part of us loves us most." We can spend our entire lives running from letting anyone see the actual condition of our soul. *If I can just keep playing the role long enough, maybe no one will catch on that I'm a mess inside.* It's true you might look better doing it that way. But you'll never know what it's like to be loved—really loved!

### Day 7: Plunder the Fear of Being Known

Do you find yourself hiding things from God? Hoping to "fake it until you make it"? Why not take a moment and let Him in? Let Him into the pain. Let Him into the dysfunction. Let Him into your past. Let Him be with *you*—not the pretend "you." See what happens. What do you have to lose? I'm guessing He won't run away when you tell Him the truth. And if you don't run away, you might find yourself drawing closer to the One who knows you best, and then come to find out He's also the One who loves you most.

**Plunder the Fear of Being Known.**

# Journal

# DAY 8
# Plunder Hope Fulfilled

---

"Believe me, dear woman, the time has come when you won't worship the Father on a mountain nor in Jerusalem, *but in your heart.*

The woman said, "*This is all so confusing*, but I do know that the Anointed One is coming—the true Messiah. And when he comes, he will tell us everything we need to know."

Jesus said to her, "You don't have to wait any longer, the Anointed One is here speaking with you—I am the One you're looking for." John 4:21, 25-26 TPT

"This is all so confusing … but the True Messiah will bring the answers." I wonder if she was leaning in when she said this? Was there something burning in her heart that hinted Jesus just might be the One she had been waiting for? Her hope is arguing with her hopelessness, and in this moment her hope wins out.

And then Jesus responds. "I am the One you're looking for. *I* am the One you're looking for. I am the *One* you're looking for. Not some other solution or random relationship. Not another husband to try and fill that bottomless whole in your soul. Not the next 'rabbi' or 'prophet' who might come along. Every sense of lack and poverty ends here. Wholly, completely, in totality, your every need is now being filled! You don't have to look any longer, don't have to chase after the wind or wait for the perfect scenario, don't have to perform one more minute."

Those words must've jolted Maridhia to her core. "I am the One." What else is there to say? She had tried desperately to have a home and a family, had even tried marriage five different times, but nothing had worked out. In the end, she had settled for living with a man, perhaps still feebly hoping, *Maybe I'll find happiness still.*

Jesus pulls no punches and minces no words. He emphatically states that He is the Messiah and the One she has been looking for. He is making all of Who He is available to her.

The moment we hear those words, everything can change. Sometimes we don't know how we got to where we are. We just know we don't want to be there anymore. Sometimes we don't know why we are where we are, but no reason is good enough to stay. And in these moments, we hear the divine whisper. "I Am the One you've been looking for. All of Who I Am is here for you, to the very depths of your greatest needs."

Would you take a moment and just listen to those words from your Savior? "I am the One you've been looking for. And I'm here now, with you, for you, and in you, if you simply let Me be."

**Plunder Hope Fulfilled.**

# Journal

# DAY 9
# Plunder Unconditional Love

---

All at once, the woman dropped her water jar and ran off to her village and told everyone, "Come and meet a man at the well who told me everything I've ever done! He could be the Anointed One we've been waiting for." Hearing this, the people came streaming out of the village to go see Jesus. (John 4:28-30 TPT)

MARIDHIA DROPS HER water jar. I love that! She drops her jar and runs back to her village. And here we see the story come full circle.

The story begins with Maridhia coming to the well to get water because she's thirsty.

She meets Jesus, who tells her He has water that will quench her thirst and overflow.

She asks for the water He just promised.

He tells her to bring her husband.

She has no husband. (*It was impossible to do what He asked.*)

By the end of the conversation, she drops her water jar—signifying her thirst had been quenched!

But when? Jesus never formally "released an impartation" over her. It never says anything about Him praying for her. She never physically drank any water. So when did she "drink" the water Jesus promised? When did she receive it?

If we take a look at when she went back to her village we can see the answer hidden in her words: "Come and meet a man at the well who told me everything I've ever done!" That's it? *"He told me everything I've ever done"?* This woman was undone because she was seen! She was undone because she was known! Jesus saw her. He really saw her. He saw her weaknesses and knew her beyond her frailties. He wasn't intimidated by her past. Instead, He called her into her divine moment, transformed her present, redeemed her past, and showed her a potential future she never thought possible.

This divine exchange happened when she met a Man who knew her condition and never ran. She met a Man who knew her best and loved her most. Her transformation was so drastic and evident that her community, the ones who "knew" her best, invited Jesus to come stay with them. *A woman who had been married five times was now leading an entire town into an encounter with Jesus!*

We know that most of the time our weakness comes from our strength overextended. Maridhia was designed with relationships as her strength. Through one conversation with Jesus, her strength was redeemed. A woman who couldn't seem to "get marriage right" became a central figure to a town on the verge of their own Jesus encounter.

> Then the Samaritans said to the woman, "We no longer believe just because of what you told us, but now we've heard him ourselves and are convinced that he really is the true Savior of the world!" (John 4:42 TPT)

Her personal story became the town's story. Her faith changed their faith. Her freedom became their freedom. Her salvation was now theirs! And her design was completely redeemed.

Let Him in. Let Him into the places you desperately need Him the most. Dare Him to show off how grand His love is for you. Dare Him to love you like His life depended on it. My guess is, He already has.

**Plunder Unconditional Love.**

# Journal

# DAY 10
## Plunder Jealousy

---

> Now Joseph had a dream, and he told *it* to his brothers; and they hated him even more. (Genesis 37:5 NKJV)

Jealousy coming from our enemies is one thing. Jealousy from close family or friends is a different kind of animal. Family is the place God designed for everyone to be celebrated. It is the refuge our dreams were meant to be launched from. Dreamers by nature live lives of uncertainty. It is what enables us to think outside the lines and try absurd, impossible feats. But that is a terrifying way to live if you can't find certainty in the home where you belong.

Home. That word conjures up a vast array of emotions. Depending on who you are speaking with, it can evoke everything from sweet to sour, sublime to terror, joy to rage, and love to fear. But it was always intended to be a sanctuary of belonging. When that is disrupted, our life of dreaming quickly loses its wings. When jealousy creeps its way into the home, then the fabric of deep relationships is torn under the horrific tension of wondering who will get their day of fulfillment and who will be left out, left behind, and left wanting?

Isn't that the root of jealousy—the sense that you'll go without something you really want? This is what makes us so frantic to control our future and fill a void that we stop thinking about people as people. They become either obstacles or commodities, those standing in the way of what we want, or a means to an end.

For the dreamer, this story feels very different. Just when the joy of life seems to be sprouting, someone else's jealousy aggressively attempts to pry the dream from our grasp and inject a syringe of bitterness into the heart of the vision. We still have the dream, but the pain attached to it can seem more than we can bear.

I have to admit I have found myself on both sides of this scenario. It's quite humbling to look back over my life and recognize moments where my jealousy kept me from celebrating what God was doing in someone else's life. Living a "hands open" life has always brought intense comfort to my soul, but it hasn't always been so easy to walk out. Even as I write this, I am fully aware that jealousy is always lurking in the shadows for an opportune moment to rob me of my joy. My prayer is that I would never be the one to cause another dreamer pain, and that if I do, I would be quick to own it, humble myself, and ask for forgiveness.

Do you find yourself wishing you had someone else's life? That could be a sign they are living out what you've only dreamt of. Do you wish they didn't have the life they are living? That's just a clear sign jealousy has sought to strangle your joy. Let it go. Humble yourself. Ask for forgiveness. Bless those you've been jealous of. Remember, most of the time it is okay to be jealous *for* what others have or are walking into. Many times that reveals something for which you were designed. Just don't fall into the trap of being jealous *of* someone else. It just doesn't look good on you. Trust me, I've tried it.

**Plunder Jealousy.**

# Journal

# DAY 11
## Plunder Rejection

---

Then Midianite traders passed by; so *the brothers* pulled Joseph up and lifted him out of the pit, and sold him to the Ishmaelites for twenty *shekels* of silver. And they took Joseph to Egypt. (Genesis 37: 28 NKJV)

Have you ever had God give you a promise and suddenly you found yourself like a porch light attracting every moth on the face of the earth? It is as if no one even cares about what you're doing until you begin to shine brighter than those around you. Instantly, adversity comes knocking, oftentimes from those closest to us. So it was with Joseph. So it is with us. *But the dream never makes us who we are. It only introduces us to ourselves.* How we repeatedly respond to life and surrender to God is what ultimately forms us.

Our brothers' jealousy will often lead to rejection. We assume our dreams will be fulfilled in the place we first dreamt them. We imagine ourselves heroes among those whose opinions we most value. Instead, obscurity can chase us down, and that in-between, no man's place can feel haunted.

Leaving one place of belonging without having our next

placed lined up shakes all that can shake. But outside the camp is where we experience God in a completely different light. There is no one else to comfort us. No one else to fill that need for belonging. Nothing familiar to us that we can rely on. We are coldly introduced to a world in which we are not king, we are not seen, we are not celebrated. We are at His mercy. And it is at His mercy we find our true selves. Here, the sweetest fragrance of His presence washes over all our senses until we are wholly His.

Rejection led to Joseph's enslavement. Yet, is it possible Joseph would never have experienced such deep growth in his character without it? Is it possible that God met him there in a way he could never have experienced elsewhere?

I encourage you to take a moment and look at the challenges in your life from a different view point. Take a moment and recognize how desperate for God you've become, how deep you've plunged into His mercy. There are always gifts we can find in adversity that we can't find in other seasons. What gift can you receive from God *because* of your challenge? What part of God are you able to get to see now that you never would've known before? Yes, even in slavery. Yes, even in rejection. Yes, even when those closest are are the ones who rejected you.

**Plunder Rejection.**

# Journal

# DAY 12
## Plunder Meaninglessness

---

Now Joseph had been taken down to Egypt. And Potiphar, an officer of Pharaoh, captain of the guard, an Egyptian, bought him from the Ishmaelites who had taken him down there. The Lord was with Joseph, and he was a successful man; and he was in the house of his master the Egyptian. And his master saw that the Lord *was* with him and that the Lord made all he did to prosper in his hand. So Joseph found favor in his sight, and served him. Then he made him overseer of his house, and all *that* he had he put under his authority. (Genesis 39:1-4 NKJV)

WHEN THE LORD is with you, success is inevitable. But success doesn't guarantee a promotion in the way we'd like. Joseph prospered while being owned by another man, and his authority increased, but not in a way we would naturally expect. He still had to contend everyday with the reality of his slavery.

Sometimes we judge if something is from God by whether or not we acquire a higher status than before. *But God values authority over status, and favor over personal position.* With God, it is possible to be in charge even while those around us see us as a slave.

Are there any areas of your life where your favor has prospered you but the fruit hasn't been the kind you'd like? You wanted the "orange" of being free to go where you want and God is producing the "banana" of influencing the people right in front of you. When this happens, sometimes we are completely blind to the fruit we *are* producing. Our eyes "go on strike" as we look for fruit everywhere other than where it actually is. We're looking for something specific, that which means most to us in our current season. God is looking for what *He* is producing, even if it looks nothing like our hopes and dreams. He is longing to produce something inside us that will last far beyond this season. And remember, He sees the entire span of our life, not just this moment.

Ask yourself this: "Where am I fruitful right now?" Don't be too quick to discard the seemingly "meaningless" places God begins to show you. What you currently find meaningless might be profound—you just don't see it yet.

**Plunder Meaninglessness.**

# Journal

# DAY 13
## Plunder Potential Bitterness

---

> So it was, from the time *that* he had made him overseer of his house and all that he had, that the Lord blessed the Egyptian's house for Joseph's sake; and the blessing of the Lord was on all that he had in the house and in the field. Thus he left all that he had in Joseph's hand, and he did not know what he had except for the bread which he ate. (Genesis 39:5-6a NKJV)

How would you handle it if the man who *bought* you ended up being blessed because of you? Is it possible that God could bless our enemy for our sake, and we just might not see it? I know "enemy" can be a strong word. A better phrase might be "those opposed to you." Potiphar doesn't appear to be a brutal slave owner. By the little that we know about him, he seems like a nice guy. But for Joseph, Potiphar was the one who bought him. Potiphar owned him. For any man, slavery is an enemy. For a man who was born free, with dreams the size of New York, his current position was far beneath anything he had imagined.

And now Joseph gets a front row seat to God overwhelming

Potiphar with blessing. God knows that if He blesses Potiphar, it will elevate Joseph in the eyes of his master. But what if Joseph had turned bitter? Maybe he actually did have some bitterness he had to fight through. We don't know. What we do know is that Joseph served with excellence, even as a slave. We also know that God blessed Joseph's enemy, and because of that blessing, Joseph was ultimately put in charge of all of Potiphar's resources.

So yes, it is possible that God will bless our enemies for our sake. The question is, will we see it? We live in a world that values the self-made and self-taught, those who follow the way of the "lone hero." In most of our stories, the heroes we revere are those who learned to do it by themselves. We in turn believe if we are really going to make it in life and fully maximize our potential, then we're going to have to make it by ourselves as well.

God's ways are not only contrary but hostile to that mindset. If we are intent on living our lives to their fullest, there is one truth for certain: we will *not* be able to walk this out on our own. Sometimes the people God has placed in our lives to move us forward can look like our worst enemy. And then, after bringing them into our lives, God sometimes has the audacity to bless them right in front of us. But if we can look past the obvious, past our pain and current condition, we might see a glimpse of reality we were blind to just a moment before.

God will bless our enemies because of us, to move us toward our destination. If we refuse to get bitter, then our moving forward will make space for our "enemies" to move with us. And as the journey begins to unfold, many who were once against us will become our friends.

Who in your life are you currently frustrated with because God is blessing them? Maybe you don't think they're worthy of it. If you dare, I challenge you to bless them yourself. Take a moment and release them from your bitterness. Is it possible that God is trying to move you forward in life, and you have turned your life into a race against the person next to you? Maybe some of your current enemies will be your future friends.

**Plunder Potential Bitterness.**

# Journal

# DAY 14
## Plunder Turmoil

---

But it happened about this time, when Joseph went into the house to do his work, and none of the men of the house *was* inside, that she caught him by his garment, saying, "Lie with me." But he left his garment in her hand, and fled and ran outside. And so it was, when she saw that he had left his garment in her hand and fled outside, that she called to the men of her house and spoke to them, saying, "See, he has brought in to us a Hebrew to mock us. He came in to me to lie with me, and I cried out with a loud voice. And it happened, when he heard that I lifted my voice and cried out, that he left his garment with me, and fled and went outside." So she kept his garment with her until his master came home. Then she spoke to him with words like these, saying, "The Hebrew servant whom you brought to us came in to me to mock me; so it happened, as I lifted my voice and cried out, that he left his garment with me and fled outside." So it was, when his master heard the words which his wife spoke to him, saying, "Your servant did to me after this manner," that his anger was aroused. Then Joseph's master took him and put him into the prison. (Genesis 39:11-20 NKJV)

**F**AVOR OPENED DOORS for Joseph and accelerated his influence even as a slave. But not every door that favor opens is from God. His influence has also set him up with the opportunity to sleep with his master's wife.

Sometimes we are positioned by God for great influence. But that influence can open us up several opportunities that are not from God at all. Our ability to say no to certain places favor has made available to us, even if it costs us our current influence, is what ultimately defines how ready we are to be trusted with what God deems valuable.

Joseph didn't have great role models in certain character issues. Abraham, Joseph's great-grandfather, had a character problem. When he first met Pharaoh, Abraham was scared for his life and lied to Pharaoh about his wife to protect himself. Isaac, Joseph's grandpa, did the same exact thing with another king, Abimelech. Jacob, Joseph's dad, consistently lied to get his way, even stealing his brother's inheritance.

Now it's Joseph's turn to decide whether he will keep his character and trust God or bend his character to save himself. He chooses the former and pays a dear price for it—he graduates from slavery to prison.

These immediate results are not what we would expect from doing things "God's way." But with God, we can't afford to judge the wisdom of our decisions from that perspective. Sometimes it takes years before we see the fruit of our character-based decisions. And sometimes it takes moments to see fruit from decisions made divorced of character.

Joseph could have slept with Potiphar's wife and might have

continued in favor with Potiphar, with the momentary fruit justifying his sin. But instead he kept his character, and in doing so broke a generational curse over his family that had been there for years! Quick fruit? No. Lasting fruit? You bet.

Is there a decision you've made where you kept your integrity, but now you question whether it was the right thing to do because it created long-term problems instead of instant solutions? Take a moment and let go of how you've judged the fruit. God knows what He's doing with your story. It just might be that your story is bigger than you. It just might be that He's looking at the entire story while you're only seeing the giants you're facing. Step back and ask God to speak hope to you again. Ask Him to comfort you and strengthen you. And ask Him to remind you that His presence in the midst of turmoil is better than false peace without Him.

**Plunder Turmoil.**

# Journal

# DAY 15
## Plunder Tension

---

> Then Joseph's master took him and put him into the prison, a place where the king's prisoners *were* confined. And he was there in the prison. But the Lord was with Joseph and showed him mercy, and He gave him favor in the sight of the keeper of the prison. And the keeper of the prison committed to Joseph's hand all the prisoners who *were* in the prison; whatever they did there, it was his doing. The keeper of the prison did not look into anything *that was* under *Joseph's* authority, because the Lord was with him; and whatever he did, the Lord made *it* prosper. (Genesis 39:20-23 NKJV)

JOSEPH WAS SENT to prison, but not just any prison. He was put where the *king's* prisoners were confined. God was positioning Joseph, even at his lowest point, to be in relationship with the right people for the right time. Again, Joseph had the favor to flourish in prison but not to get out of prison. He prospered, and his authority once again increased. Authority and integrity combined to give him radical kingdom influence even in prison. His gifts and skill set developed, and his character matured. Everything he touched prospered. God's hand stayed on him, and Joseph responded by walking out his everyday tasks with uncommon excellence.

There is a divine tension in seeing your favor increase while your position hits a ceiling. Something quite extraordinary starts to grow in moments like that. It forces you to dig a little deeper, rest a little harder, and push a little stronger. There is no room for getting your identity from your current condition. If we entertain that kind of thinking—allowing our condition to define us—then when it's time to be prime minister, to fulfill the role we're preparing for, we won't be ready. We'll always be afraid of losing control of our circumstances, as if those circumstances *do* define us. Our thinking must be free before our circumstances are free. Joseph epitomized this truth.

Do you know how that feels? To have something stirring in you but no platform to release it fully? If so, how are you responding? Are you going deeper in God or have you let the fire burn out so you don't have to deal with the tension anymore? Take some time and let God spark your fire again. Take your frustrations to Him and watch your mind get transformed in preparation for the fullness of your calling.

**Plunder Tension.**

# Journal

# DAY 16
## Plunder the Mundane

---

Then the butler and the baker of the king of Egypt, who *were* confined in the prison, had a dream, both of them, each man's dream in one night *and* each man's dream with its *own* interpretation. And Joseph came in to them in the morning and looked at them, and saw that they *were* sad. So he asked Pharaoh's officers who *were* with him in the custody of his lord's house, saying, "Why do you look *so* sad today?"

And they said to him, "We each have had a dream, and *there is* no interpreter of it."

So Joseph said to them, "Do not interpretations belong to God? Tell *them* to me, please."

Now [after Joseph interpreted their dreams] it came to pass on the third day, *which was* Pharaoh's birthday, that he made a feast for all his servants; and he lifted up the head of the chief butler and of the chief baker among his servants. Then he restored the chief butler to his butlership again, and he placed the cup in Pharaoh's hand. But he hanged the chief baker, as Joseph had interpreted to them. (Genesis 40:5-8, 20-22 NKJV)

**B**EING POSITIONED NEXT to people of influence creates opportunities for God to shine through you. Joseph was quick to give God credit for his ability to interpret the butler's and baker's dreams. But without Joseph's availability and willingness to take a risk, neither of the men would have seen the power of God that day. What would have happened if Joseph had been thinking like a prisoner instead of a prince? He might have missed the broad door of God's favor standing right in front of him.

Remember, Joseph's personal dreams were more about him and his family. But his gift to interpret dreams were about everyone else around him. He had yet to see how this could all flow together in the plans of God, yet it didn't stop him from helping those in his immediate path. He knew that his current circumstances (prison) and his current condition (prisoner) couldn't hold him back from God's plan. So, he took the opportunity right in front of him instead of waiting for the perfect scenario.

Are you at a moment in your life where it is impossible to see how God will bring everything together? Do you find yourself miles from the dream God placed inside of you? Maybe there aren't any open doors in front of you that appear to lead to your dream, but has God placed any seemingly insignificant doors in front of you? If so, why not go through them and see what happens? Sometimes your shortest pathway is hidden in the mundane.

**Plunder the Mundane.**

# Journal

# DAY 17
## Plunder Delay

---

Yet the chief butler did not remember Joseph, but forgot him …

Then it came to pass, at the end of two full years, that Pharaoh had a dream;

In the morning his mind was troubled, so he sent for all the magicians and wise men of Egypt. Pharaoh told them his dreams, but no one could interpret them for him.

Then the chief cupbearer said to Pharaoh, "Today I am reminded of my shortcomings. Pharaoh was once angry with his servants, and he imprisoned me and the chief baker in the house of the captain of the guard. Each of us had a dream the same night, and each dream had a meaning of its own. Now a young Hebrew was there with us, a servant of the captain of the guard. We told him our dreams, and he interpreted them for us, giving each man the interpretation of his dream. 13 And things turned out exactly as he interpreted them to us: I was restored to my position, and the other man was impaled."

So Pharaoh sent for Joseph, and he was quickly brought from the dungeon. When he had shaved and changed his clothes, he came before Pharaoh. (Genesis 40:23, 41:1a,8-14NKJV)

Being forgotten isn't the worst thing that can happen to us. Even when we have clarity of calling, we often lack clarity of timing. I've found that God can actually give people momentary amnesia of our gifts and influence. This is not punishment, but His mercy that keeps us from going through a door that is not yet ready for us. Remember, our gifts will open many doors. But that doesn't necessarily mean that the people on the other side of those doors are ready to receive what we have to give. Nor does it mean that we are fully ready to carry the weight that comes on the other side of our gifts in full display.

"At the end of two full years." That's an interesting phrase. There was a "fullness" to what needed to transpire before Pharaoh was ready for Joseph. What exactly needed to shift? We don't know. But we do know that the butler's momentary amnesia was a part of God's plan.

So what do we focus on when we are being forgotten? It is a very real thing to experience, and it doesn't always feel great when it's happening. I'm thankful there is a treasure inevitably waiting for us when we are invisible to the people around us. When we are invisible to people, we get the chance to experience being fully seen by God. Not that He doesn't always see us. But when applause from people is absent we are a sponge for the applause of God. He doesn't disappoint.

What if you were to enjoy your "invisibility" rather than disdain it? There is a sweetness to those moments of *aloneness* with God where the bustle of clamoring voices begins to fade. There are nuances of His voice that your ears begin to pick up. Take a moment and surrender the places in your life that are on "pause" or have been delayed. It just might be His mercy taking you deeper into Him.

**Plunder Delay.**

# Journal

# DAY 18
## Plunder Brokenness

---

So Pharaoh sent for Joseph, and he was quickly brought from the dungeon. When he had shaved and changed his clothes, he came before Pharaoh.

Pharaoh said to Joseph, "I had a dream, and no one can interpret it. But I have heard it said of you that when you hear a dream you can interpret it."

"I cannot do it," Joseph replied to Pharaoh, "but God will give Pharaoh the answer he desires." (Genesis 41:14-16 NIV)

Brokenness comes with a price, but the fruit is irrefutable. This could've been the moment for Joseph to finally shine and make a name for himself. After years in slavery and prison, at last he is standing in front of a king. What will he do? Show off? Make himself indispensable? Sell his wisdom to the highest bidder? Or simply yield to God, worship Him only, and shift the attention of Pharaoh to the source of Joseph's wisdom?

We read the rest of the story and see that the way Joseph handled this worked out great for him. But put yourself in his shoes. You've now spent thirteen years of your life in slavery and prison. Every time you've been promoted, something has disrupted your promotion and sent you into deeper turmoil. If there was ever a time to make sure you stood out, it would be this moment. The gift God has given you will certainly set you apart. There's no need to even give a hint that God is the One giving you wisdom. Take the credit and get out of prison. You'll have plenty of time to point to God once you're a success. After all, keeping your character has only bent your trajectory into a downward spiral from bad to worse.

But brokenness has a voice that shatters pride. There's nothing left for Joseph to prove. He has learned the art of complete surrender. He's learned to live in an authority far above his circumstances. Trading that kind of authority for momentary recognition would be absurd. While in prison, Joseph learned to rest in the hands of God. This will now afford him the wisdom to stay under God's mighty hand even if it means staying in prison.

And so Joseph makes it clear to Pharaoh where his wisdom comes from. "I cannot do it," Joseph replied to Pharaoh, "but God will give Pharaoh the answer he desires." It's simple. Joseph redirects Pharaoh's attention to God, fully revealing that he is completely at the mercy of God. Any solution to Pharaoh's problems will not be used to puff up Joseph's ego. They'll only be used to bring glory to God.

How incredible is it to find yourself in such a sweet spot of brokenness, the place where you cannot be bought off by popular opinion, favor with powerful people, or some promise of a better future. God is the *best future*! He is not second best. Being with God in any circumstance is far better than being without Him in the 'best of circumstances." Joseph knew this, and so do we.

Puffing up our own ego is not a benign act. It inserts the cancer of pride into our self-perception. When we try to feel powerful by stroking our ego, it leads us to isolation and a life of striving. But brokenness teaches us that surrender is the key to not lacking anything, while striving in our own strength is the key to habitually lacking everything.

Take a moment and look at areas of your life you feel you need to strive in your own strength. Compare them to places of complete surrender. What is the difference in the fruit of those areas? Where would you like to grow in surrender? Spend some time with God and ask Him for wisdom.

**Plunder Brokenness.**

# Journal

# DAY 19
## Plunder Pressure

---

So now let Pharaoh seek out *and* provide a man discreet, understanding, proficient, *and* wise and set him over the land of Egypt [as governor]. Let Pharaoh do this; then let him select and appoint officers over the land, and take one-fifth [of the produce] of the [whole] land of Egypt in the seven plenteous years [year by year]. And let them gather all the food of these good years that are coming and lay up grain under the direction *and* authority of Pharaoh, and let them retain food [in fortified granaries] in the cities. And that food shall be put in store for the country against the seven years of hunger *and* famine that are to come upon the land of Egypt, so that the land may not be ruined *and* cut off by the famine.

And the plan seemed good in the eyes of Pharaoh and in the eyes of all his servants. And Pharaoh said to his servants, Can we find this man's equal, a man in whom is the spirit of God?

And Pharaoh said to Joseph, Forasmuch as [your] God has shown you all this, there is nobody as intelligent *and* discreet *and* understanding and wise as you are. You shall have charge over my house, and all my people shall be governed according to your word [with reverence, submission, and obedience]. Only in matters of the throne will I be greater than you are. (Genesis 41:33-40 AMPC)

God's favor stands Joseph in front of Pharaoh. But Joseph's character, experience, skill set, and endurance give him the tools to administrate, implement, and govern the immense project Pharaoh's dream produced.

The favor of God will often open several doors in front of us, yet, it takes wisdom to steward the opportunities favor brings us. And it takes character and skill to sustain the stewardship that wisdom has outlined. While favor, our gift, and even moments of wisdom can be given to us, character and skill are developed through time.

Imagine for a moment finding yourself in a high-rise in downtown New York. You have an appointment on the thirty-fifth floor. As you step into the elevator, Bill Gates also steps in. His destination is the forty-fifth floor. On your way up, you overhear him sharing with his companions a dream he had the night before. In a moment, you completely understand the dream and its interpretation. With boldness you share with him the interpretation and the wisdom and strategy for what to do next.

At this point, most of what you've given Mr. Gates has come fairly easily. It took courage to speak up. It took some years of experience to gain the wisdom. But oftentimes, a gift of wisdom and counsel is sufficient for moments like these.

But as you start to get off on the thirty-fifth floor, Mr. Gates stops you. "I've never seen someone who understands the way you do," he says. "I'd like you to come and facilitate the strategy you just gave me."

## Day 19: Plunder Pressure

That's when the weight of responsibility drops. Your gift opened a door, your wisdom walked you through it. But only your character will sustain you for the full length of years required to facilitate the dream. And character doesn't come cheap.

Joseph's favor was prominent from the time he was a youngster. His ability to have dreams and interpret them came with ease. But his ability to facilitate and administrate Pharaoh's dream came with a very steep price. It was only in slavery and prison that Joseph gained the skills, character, and wherewithal to brilliantly lead an entire nation through a famine. Joseph's courage and insight positioned Pharaoh to prosper when everyone else was on the edge of survival.

Likewise, your favor and gifts will open many doors to help bring meaningful solutions and answers to other people's problems. That can be exhilarating. But it is the things developed in you when nothing seems to be going right, when no one notices you, when your gifts are put on the back burner and your brilliance hidden, that you develop the character and skill sets needed to truly lead people through their own famines. As the late John Wooden said, "Ability may get you to the top, but it takes character to keep you there."

Instead of regretting your years in "slavery" and "prison," maybe it's time to be thankful for all that was developed in those intense moments of pressure, to be thankful for all you now have, and notice how much of it God gave you *while* you were still in a dark place. That's what plundering your darkness is all about.

**Plunder Pressure.**

# Journal

# DAY 20
# Plunder Disappointment In Dreams

---

Now Joseph had a dream, and he told *it* to his brothers; and they hated him even more. So he said to them, "Please hear this dream which I have dreamed: 7 There we were, binding sheaves in the field. Then behold, my sheaf arose and also stood upright; and indeed your sheaves stood all around and bowed down to my sheaf." And his brothers said to him, "Shall you indeed reign over us? Or shall you indeed have dominion over us?" So they hated him even more for his dreams and for his words. (Genesis 37:5-8 NKJV)

Now Joseph was the governor of the land, the person who sold grain to all its people. So when Joseph's brothers arrived, they bowed down to him with their faces to the ground. (Genesis 42:6 NIV)

JOSEPH'S ORIGINAL DREAM revealed that one day his brothers would bow down to him. Here, twenty-plus years later, the dream is fulfilled. The path that took Joseph to the fulfillment of his dream was, I'm sure, completely different than the one he had expected. But the journey also provided the preparation to see the dream fulfilled in the way that God intended.

Remember, we usually see our dreams through the lens of how we'll look, feel, and succeed. But God looks through a holistic lens. He sees how the dream will affect everyone around us, and what will ultimately show off His glory to a world in desperate need of our incredible God.

By the time Joseph's dream is fulfilled, he no longer has the stomach for a world that revolves around his ego. The fact that his brothers are finally bowing down to him isn't a moment for "I told you so." He isn't looking for that kind of affirmation. Egotistical drive has been beaten out of him. Instead, the dream fulfilled is actually the doorway to seeing his entire family saved from a famine! But what was the final key to unlocking this story? What positioned him for a fulfilled life and the privilege to save his own family?

The answer to that question is the answer to many others as well. Joseph spent time interpreting and stewarding someone else's dream. It was in the stewarding of Pharaoh's dream that Joseph's dream was realized.

Serving those around us and partnering with them to see their dreams become a reality is one of the grandest privileges we have in this life. It is also the secret to seeing our dreams fulfilled in a way that is meaningful, not futile.

Most of the time we're told to pursue our dreams at any cost. How self-defeating is that? In the midst of us chasing our dreams, we could be passing by the very people God has sent into our lives so our dreams can fully manifest. After all, aren't the greatest dreams in life the ones about people? Isn't it all supposed to be about people? Don't buy into the lie that "something" will fill a void inside of you. "Something" can never give you what

## Day 20: Plunder Disappointment In Dreams

"Someone" can. And remember, your dream isn't just about you. If it is, then it's shallow, petty, and worthless. By all means, get a new dream!

Think about the people right in front of you. Who has God placed in your life? What if you took a healthy portion of your energy and put it into seeing their dreams fulfilled? Is it possible that yours would move a couple steps forward in the process? I know sometimes we can't see it. And there are no guarantees. Maybe your dream will stay stuck. But one guarantee is certain: If you lend your strength to those around you, you'll love them well. And at that point, you'll win no matter what.

**Plunder Disappointment In Dreams.**

# Journal

# DAY 21
# Plunder Pain

---

And Joseph said to his brothers, I am Joseph! Is my father still alive? And his brothers could not reply, for they were distressingly disturbed and dismayed at [the startling realization that they were in] his presence.

And Joseph said to his brothers, Come near to me, I pray you. And they did so. And he said, I am Joseph your brother, whom you sold into Egypt! But now, do not be distressed and disheartened or vexed and angry with yourselves because you sold me here, for God sent me ahead of you to preserve life. For these two years the famine has been in the land, and there are still five years more in which there will be neither plowing nor harvest. God sent me before you to preserve for you a posterity and to continue a remnant on the earth, to save your lives by a great escape and save for you many survivors. So now it was not you who sent me here, but God; and He has made me a father to Pharaoh and lord of all his house and ruler over all the land of Egypt. Hurry and go up to my father and tell him, Your son Joseph says this to you: God has put me in charge of all Egypt. Come down to me; do not delay. You will live in the land of Goshen, and you will be close to me—you and your children and your grandchildren, your flocks, your herds, and all you have. And there I will sustain and provide for you, so that you and your household and all that are yours may not come to poverty and want, for there are yet five [more] years of [the scarcity, hunger, and starvation of] famine. Now notice! Your own eyes and the eyes of my brother Benjamin can see that I am talking to you personally [in your language and not through an interpreter]. And you shall tell my father of all my glory in Egypt and of all that you have seen; and you shall hurry and bring my father down here. (Genesis 45:3-13 AMPC)

THE PAIN OF rejection can go so deep, it can plague us for the rest of our lives. Rejection would like to scream in our face, "You are not worthy of love. You'll never belong! There is something inherently wrong with you."

Thirteen years in slavery and prison is a long time to stew in those types of thoughts and emotions, and I'm sure Joseph struggled with them all. If they had found a place to settle, they certainly would have festered until bitterness took over. But somewhere along the journey, Joseph must've made a different choice, because what comes out of him when he is finally reunited with his brothers is not bitterness. Quite the opposite. Forgiveness, understanding, and insight into God's masterplan are all Joseph can talk about.

He had obviously worked it out with God. Because he chose forgiveness instead of bitterness, the original dream about his brothers and family bowing to him became the beginning of the story instead of the end of the story.

Imagine if Joseph had not taken the forgiveness road. When

## Day 21: Plunder Pain

Joseph's brothers came and bowed before him, Joseph could have put them in prison and moved on his merry way. He could even have justified it and used the "dream" God gave him to imprison his own family. "God showed me when I was young that my family would bow to me. This must be what God wants." If he had taken this route, all would have been lost. The fulfillment of God's ultimate plan would have taken a major detour.

Instead, the "dream" of his brothers bowing to him simply represents the beginning steps of his entire family being rescued from a famine and Joseph's place in the family being completely restored and solidified. They would spend the rest of their lives together in Egypt, and Joseph would be reunited with his father Jacob. Because Joseph refused to get bitter, he was able to pave the way for those who had hurt him the deepest to be blessed the most. That is true freedom.

How about you? Who has hurt you? Have you ever been rejected? Felt betrayed by the ones who were supposed to protect you? All of us have. But is it possible that in God's greater plan He has positioned you to move forward into your freedom first? Not to cut them off, but to build a place and break open the door so they might find freedom as well?

This is the privilege of those of us who are surrendered to Christ. We are so free we can find great pleasure in making a way for those who've hurt us the worst to be forgiven, set free, and restored. When we experience the joy of giving our treasure away, plundering darkness becomes a way of life.

**Plunder Pain.**

# Journal

# The Journey Continues

You've completed your first round of the 21-Day *Plunder Darkness* experience. I trust you discovered things about you, God, and your community that you might not have known before.

Which days meant most to you? Where could you see yourself? Others? God? I'd love to hear your stories. If you'd like to share, please email me at craig@craigmuster.com

As you might've already guessed, *Plunder Darkness* isn't about visiting freedom—it is about living in freedom! It is the promise of a lifestyle of constant, deep, restorative redemption. We experience loss every day. We experience pain every day. But what if our lives were not defined by loss or pain, but rather the redemption power of Jesus Christ to restore our hearts and lives—not merely on an occasional basis, but as a lifestyle? How would your life look if it was redeemed on a daily, hourly, or even moment-by-moment basis? How much would you see the majesty of God in a lifestyle like that? I don't know, but I'd like to find out! Would you go with me on this journey? Let's spend the rest of our lives surrendering to the majesty of the only One worthy of our whole hearts, lives, dreams, and aspirations!

I encourage you to invite others on the journey with you.

Launch 21-Day *Plunder Darkness* micro-communities. Make freedom contagious!

In closing, I like to finish the story I described in the introduction about the gold mine . The story didn't stop there. The mine began to produce so much gold that it became fully operational again and is still active to this day. In addition, because of the discovery of the new method of mining, the miners now had the courage to go back to shafts where they had stopped mining and begin digging fresh shafts once again. This led to one of the most profitable discoveries. Just fifty feet from where they had stopped digging decades before, they found the "mother lode"! Not only were they discovering minuscule flakes of gold in piles of dirt, but they were also finding large veins of gold in plain sight.

May it be so in your life. As you experience the joy of finding gold in your piles of dirt, may it give you the courage to return to places you stopped digging and once again push just a little further. Who knows—you just might find yourself fifty feet from the greatest treasures for which your heart has longed.

# Journal

# About the Author

CRAIG MUSTER IS an international speaker and author of Plunder Darkness. His passion to *awaken fierce leaders* spans multiple platforms from Executive Life and Business Coaching, International Conference Speaking, Pastoring and Leadership Development.

As an author, international speaker, song writer, church planter, business owner and creative, his life experience combined with unique communication skills translate into riveting, substantive work that creates momentum and produces real change.

Craig provokes deep, meaningful living, focusing on Identity (who you are), Community (who you belong to), and Unique Expression (how you love your world).

Craig currently resides in San Diego, CA with the love of his life, Karlet, and his three beautiful children Bella, Sophia, and Moses.

If you'd like to book Craig and/or Karlet for a speaking engagement visit www.craigandkarlet.com

Craig also offers in-depth **Plunder Darkness Masterminds**, personally taking you, along with a group of *fierce leaders*, through your story of *Plundering Darkness*. You can visit www.craigmuster.com for more information about current Masterminds as well as Executive and Team coaching.

Leave an amazon review and join the facebook group Plunder Darkness to share your story of how you are plundering darkness! We'd love to hear from you.

Made in the USA
Middletown, DE
22 September 2023

38938212R00064